A Woman's Guide to

Personal Achievement
& Professional Success

A Woman's Guide to

Personal Achievement
& Professional Success

How to make meaningful choices and changes to create the life you want

by Tami West

SkillPath Publications

Editor: Bill Cowles

Layout and cover design: Jason Sprenger and Jason Dill

ISBN: 978-1-934589-51-9

10 9 8 7 6 5 4 3 2   07   08   09   10

Printed in the United States of America

Table of Contents

Introduction

Are you anything like Susan?

Susan was a flight attendant for a major international airline. Because she is a natural people pleaser, she looked forward to each flight. She loved to see the new faces as well as the familiar ones. She enjoyed the hustle and bustle of the airports. She loved the thrill of take-off and landing. She relished the flexibility in her schedule and always accepted last-minute requests to fly to new places.

Because of Susan's work ethic and commitment, she was offered a promotion as a Base Manager, which she accepted enthusiastically. It is a very prestigious position and offered a 15% pay raise. Susan now works in a beautiful office, managing all of the flight attendants at a very busy airport. She meets regularly with other airline managers to keep the in-flight department running smoothly.

Two months into the position Susan was feeling miserable. She found herself to be resentful of the people she managed. The paperwork was overwhelming. The meetings seemed pointless and time-consuming. She was having difficulty with working the daily 9 a.m. to 5 p.m. grind.

Her friends and family noticed a change in Susan's usual positive outlook. What happened?

Susan's story isn't unusual—change the industry and titles and it very well could be yours or mine. We want it all and think we have to do it all. We work hard to prove ourselves to our bosses, our spouses, our friends, our parents and our children. We want to do an excellent job, have a clean house, well-behaved children and a fabulous marriage.

So, is it possible to have it all? To do it all? To be everything to everyone? Not exactly—at least not the way you may be currently defining "all" and "everything."

Changing your perceptions means changing your life. You already have the ability to have it all. You may just not know it yet.

Everything about your nature as a woman can work together to give you the life you've always dreamed of. You are pre-wired with mechanisms that can help you to control your stress. Women crave relationships, and when you nurture them you feel more balanced. You have been given the gift of communication. Use it to feel complete. You can choose excellence over perfection to repair your self-esteem.

I hope you use this book for three purposes:

- To evaluate how you *are* living your life
- To determine how you *want* to live your life
- To make choices to begin living the life you want

My desire is for you to find what I have found. A life filled with the joys you are meant to have. A life in which you use *everything* you have been given until, at the end, you have nothing left!

Tami

—Tami West

Chapter One:

Balance: What Does It Mean?

In 1963, Betty Friedan's controversial book *The Feminine Mystique* told of suburban housewives "taking tranquilizers like cough drops." Why? According to Friedan, it was due to discontent with their roles as wives and mothers. They wanted more.

Friedan wrote because she identified with these women. She felt a need to help rescue them from their plight. Did it help? Most certainly in many ways it did. But did this "liberation" from the home cure the anxieties and depression? Nope. Still there.

Fast forward to 1999—the discontent was still there when Susan Lewis wrote *Reinventing Ourselves After Motherhood*. Lewis, like Friedan, noticed that many women were just unhappy. But now, according to Lewis, their unhappiness was due to having the "more" discussed by Friedan. Now women had the life outside of the home—they had careers. Lewis says, "All the women with whom I spoke had stories; stories filled with conflict, anger, doubt, love, guilt, denial, ambition, confusion, pride."

So where does that leave us? We cannot be placed into one large group labeled "women." We differ in intelligence, desires, talents, skills and lifestyles. Some are single. Some are married. Some have young children, some older. Some are raising grandchildren, and some are caring for aging parents. And yet we all have something in common. A desire for balance. A desire for peace.

We all want it. Barbara Ehrenreich, biologist, author and columnist, says that: "Meaningful work and a balanced life are deep rooted and genuine human needs. Like any needs they can be repressed or ignored for years at a time, but sooner or later they're going to assert themselves." It's time to stop ignoring them.

You are looking for change in your life. But what kind of change are you looking for? By choosing this book, you have indicated that there is something about your life that you do not like. Something is "out of balance." It is crucial to begin your journey with a statement of your vision. And it is important to do this now, before you begin this life-changing endeavor.

My vision of work/life balance is: _____

_____

_____

My goal in completing this study is: _____

_____

_____

What do women want from work?

In her book *Be Happy at Work: 100 Women Who Love Their Jobs, and Why*, Joanne Gordon defines happiness at work as, "being engaged in activities whose outcomes you are proud of and with people you respect." She contends that "There are no happy jobs. There are only happy workers."

Why do you work? What do you want from work? Be completely honest.

I work because:_____

_____

_____

My vision of how I would like my work to be:_____

_____

_____

What do women want from life?

In her book *When Work Doesn't Work Anymore*, Elizabeth Perle McKenna explains that all of the women she interviewed "wanted more time for family and friends, and less stress. Most felt they were making too little contribution to their communities."

My vision of how I would like my personal life to be is: _____

_____

_____

Are you sure you know what you want?

Many workers believe the most important factor in accepting a promotion is monetary compensation, with the second most important being prestige. What most people don't do is consider their values when making life-changing decisions.

Ivy Haley says this about the importance of values in *Discovering Your Purpose*: "Having a ready grasp of your values allows you to focus on direction and purpose; otherwise, you'll likely experience conflict, manage your time poorly, and make decisions in a somewhat random fashion."

So, what are your values? What's important to you?

Think of activities that you participate in throughout the day that bring you pleasure. These could be at work, at home or outside the home. Don't be limited in your thinking. For example, you might enjoy watching a particular television show, drawing, taking a walk, talking on the phone, "crunching" numbers or even shopping.

I feel very content when I am (list up to five):

1. _____

2. _____

3. _____

4. _____

5. _____

Now try to attach a reason to your happiness during these times. For example, do you enjoy your Tuesday night television shows because you can spend time with your family, because you can spend time alone or for some other reason? Maybe you have multiple reasons why you enjoy an activity. Try to find at least one reason for each activity you listed.

1. _____

2. _____

3. _____

4. _____

5. _____

Typically, we feel the most joy when we are doing something that aligns with what we value. We feel discontent and guilt when we are not.

On the following page is a list of values. It is certainly not exhaustive, and you may add to it. When doing a values assessment, it is important to do three things. First, allow yourself plenty of time. Next, take the "shoulds" out of your mind. Maybe you grew up in a family that was very competitive, so you believe you should also be competitive even though you aren't. And finally, ask yourself this question for each value you select: *What in my life demonstrates that I value this?*

Directions:

1. Think about why you enjoy the activities you listed. You will probably find something you value. Use this information to begin your values assessment. Choose ten that are important to you. Number them 1 to 10 in the "Initial Assessment" column (not necessarily in order of importance). Make sure you describe what you do in your life that demonstrates this.

2. Now, narrow down your list of ten to your five core values. Number them 1 to 5 in the "core values" column (again, not necessarily in order of importance). Two suggestions for doing this are:

   - If you had trouble or couldn't come up with a demonstration, it may not be a value (or maybe you're just not living to your values)

   - Ask yourself "Which values can I not live without?"

Core values	Initial assessment	Value	What I do in my life that demonstrates the importance of this value
		Achievement	
		Action	
		Appreciation	
		Authenticity	
		Autonomy	
		Challenge	
		Competition	
		Creativity	
		Flexibility	
		Freedom	
		Growth	
		Helping	
		Humor	
		Independence	
		Influence	
		Integrity	
		Leading	
		Predictability	
		Public contact	
		Relaxed pace	
		Respect	
		Responsibility	
		Risk	
		Security	
		Status	
		Teamwork	
		Trust	
		Variety	

Think back to our opening scenario with Susan. She valued action, freedom, flexibility and helping. Yet she accepted a position in which she was unable to experience any of these.

Consider your values, your job and your life in general. Below, list each value and place a check mark in one or both columns as appropriate.

My Core Values	✓ I live to this value at home	✓ I live to this value at work

One way to feel a sense of balance in your life is to incorporate what you say you value. It's okay if you didn't place a check mark in every column. For example, maybe you love your job even though it isn't very flexible—one of your top values. What's important is that you find ways to incorporate that value in your personal life.

In the spaces on the following page, for each of your values that is not currently integrated into your lifestyle, write one action statement regarding how you will change that and make it part of your life.

Action steps:

I will incorporate _____ into my life by: _____

_____

_____

I will incorporate _____ into my life by: _____

_____

_____

I will incorporate _____ into my life by: _____

_____

_____

I will incorporate _____ into my life by: _____

_____

_____

You now have spent some time with the most important areas of your life:

- What does balance mean to you?
- Why are you working on this area of your life?
- Why do you work?
- What do you want out of work?
- What do you want out of your personal life?
- What are your values?
- Are your actions consistent with those values?
- If they are not, what are you going to do to change that?

Your work begins now

Now it's time to examine six areas of your life that affect your perception of balance. They are all related to being a woman. They all will be life-changing if you let them.

These are the six areas you will focus on:

1. Your nature as a woman

2. Stress control

3. Relationships

4. Communication

5. Perfectionism and guilt

6. Time and organization

As you work through each of these areas, refer back to your original definition of balance and what you want to accomplish. Re-examine what you said you want out of work and out of life in general. Refer back to how your values affect each area of your life. Your definitions, expectations and perceptions are likely to change.

The search for balance is not just about time management. It's more about attitude. When we stop looking at our external circumstances as dictating our lives and start looking inside ourselves, *that's* when the real change begins!

Chapter Two:

The Privilege of Being a Woman

Understanding gender differences

Samantha works full time as an administrative assistant at an electrical manufacturing company. She is married and has two children, ages three and six. Her aunt is temporarily living with her family to help take care of the children.

Anna is Samantha's best friend and confidante, but she is growing weary of Samantha's constant complaining. Their most recent conversation left Anna feeling frustrated and confused. As usual, Samantha's complaint went something like this: "No one ever does anything around here! They expect me to do it all! I really hate my life. I hate my job. My boss treats me like a second class citizen, John never does anything with the kids and I've about had it!"

Anna has heard it all before—many times. But her advice to Samantha is always dismissed.

"Why don't you talk to everyone about working together?" Anna suggests.

"That will never work," Samantha replies.

"Can you work on adjusting your hours at work?" Anna continues.

"Nope. We can't afford it." She hears.

And the conversation continues this way. In Samantha's eyes, there is no solution.

Sound familiar? It is impossible to speak of work/life balance without including a discussion of our nature as women. So many women are made angry by the very traits that come along with being female. Women are created with certain strengths and weaknesses. Men are created with certain strengths and weaknesses.

Consider the traditional role of men in society—breadwinner. Right? Cynthia Culver, author of *Points West Magazine* (a publication of the Buffalo Bill Historical Center), says this about men's roles on the Oregon frontier during the mid 1860's: "Oregonians expected men at least to appear to provide for their families without assistance from their wives, and they were highly critical of men who failed to do so. They expected men to support their families with their field labor, allowing their wives to focus on their domestic role."

Have men's roles changed much in the past 100 or so years? David Maume, University of Cincinnati sociologist, Kunz Center Director and author of the *Survey of Ohio's Working Families*, said: "Men's contribution to household chores has changed little from earlier decades, when husbands' share of housework was estimated at 20 – 25 percent."

Carefully consider the following, then:

1. What do *you* believe the role of men is in society today? _____

_____

_____

_____

2. Think of a significant male in your life. This could be your boss, husband, boyfriend, father, etc. Describe the ideal role he should play in your life (e.g., how you would like him to behave, what you would like him to do). _____

_____

_____

_____

Now consider the traditional role of women in society—caretaker. Right? Culver says the belief was that "wives should remain at home, managing the domestic work and raising children."

Have women's roles changed much in the past 100 years? According to Maume, "many women work full time during the day, and then work a 'second shift' of household chores at night."

Carefully consider the following:

1. What do *you* believe the role of women is in society today? _____

   _____

   _____

   _____

2. Describe your idea of your role as the woman in your home and/or at work (e.g., what should you be primarily responsible for?) _____

   _____

   _____

   _____

Having considered the realities of the roles of men and women, now let's look at the way each gender is "wired." What is in our very basic nature? Here are some "fun facts":

- We all have sex chromosomes. Females have two X chromosomes. Males have one X and one Y.
- A 2006 study at the University of Virginia found an association between the Y chromosome and aggressive behavior. They also found the absence of the Y to be associated with maternal behavior.

So, what does this mean? We often fail to recognize that we are absolutely biologically different! Because of this, we think differently, we communicate differently and we have different ideas about our roles at home and at work. This should not be synonymous with misery.

1. You are at work when a fire breaks out. It seems as if everyone is safely evacuated when you hear a scream from just inside the first floor. Who goes in after the person?

   [Man]   [Woman]

2. You just gave birth to your first child. You and your husband are blissfully happy. Who stays home with the baby?

   [Man]   [Woman]

3. You and your husband are having major financial difficulties even though you both work full-time. You have two children. Who gets a second job?

   [Man]   [Woman]

4. A co-worker of yours has been diagnosed with cancer. You work in a large department, and not everyone knows each other. Everyone is trying to decide what to do to help. Several of you decide to put together a quilt with a handwritten note patch from each employee. This will be useful during chemotherapy for warmth and to occupy time. Who heads up this quilt-making committee?

   [Man]   [Woman]

Your answers to these questions may reflect the true beliefs that you hold about the roles of men and women. Your views are shaped by your past experiences. At the very least, it is important to recognize that we should value our strengths and work together. Culver recognized this about families on the Oregon frontier: "Even the most successful farmers relied on a partnership between themselves and their wives to make their farms run smoothly." Partnership. At home and at work—that's the key. So, what can you do? Here are five simple steps to reconciling your feelings about being a woman:

1. Make a list of the joys you experience because you are a woman. Post these somewhere to remind you when you are feeling overwhelmed.

2. Make a list of your challenges. Beside each challenge write a possible solution.

3. If you work in a gender-mixed environment, consider setting up a seminar to educate everyone on gender differences and how you can be "partners."

4. At home, script out conversations to have with your family members. Let go of your anger and your expectations about what others "should" do. This is not effective and will lead to more frustration and less balance. (More about scripting in another chapter.)

   Remember Samantha? Instead of saying something like, *"You never help me,"* she might say something like this: *"Yesterday after dinner I cleaned up the entire kitchen by myself. When things like that happen I feel frustrated because I think you assume it's my job. I appreciate all that you do at work. I would really like for us to clean up the kitchen together."* (Notice, no "buts.")

5. Finally, never give up and fall into the "no solution" trap. There is *always* a solution.

Estrogen and emotions

The feelings that accompany estrogen fluctuations are *real*. They are very different from simply being in a bad mood. What does estrogen do, anyway?

- Studies show that estrogen enhances our response to stress. This may help to explain why women are twice as likely to experience anxiety and depression as men.

- Estrogen is associated with mood changes. Two common patterns are PMS (Premenstrual Syndrome) and PMDD (Premenstrual Dysphoric Disorder—a more severe form of PMS). The presence of these conditions, as well as the severity of symptoms, varies from woman to woman.

The problem is, we are not always in touch with the difference, and when the emotions arrive we are not prepared. There are two steps you can take to be prepared:

1. The first step in this preparation is to keep an "Emotions Log" for a minimum of two months. Begin the log on the first day of your period, and end it on the first day of your next period. This step is crucial, but often women are resistant because they do not like admitting to this aspect of their lives.

   Include the following information in each entry:

   - Physical symptoms (e.g., cramping, bloating, headaches, etc.):
   - Emotions (e.g., happy, angry, sad, etc.):
   - Events associated with each emotion:
   - My actions associated with each event:

   At the end of each month, notice any emotional fluctuations you experienced. Some form of PMS occurs in approximately 75% of women. The physical symptoms may include:

   - Swelling
   - General aches and pains
   - Nausea
   - Diarrhea or constipation
   - Headache

   The emotional symptoms may include:

   - Mood swings
   - Crying
   - Nervousness
   - Irritability
   - Difficulty concentrating
   - Forgetfulness
   - Anger
   - Confusion

   Depending on the severity of your symptoms, you may want to discuss possible treatment options with your doctor.

2. The next step must be to take action! Here are six very specific ways to alleviate some of the stress that may come along on your high-estrogen days. Implementing these may alter your perception of workload and home responsibilities.

— **Have a "physical survival kit" available at home and at work.** The kit may include such items as:

- Pain reliever (aspirin, etc.)
- Feminine hygiene products
- Soothing essential oils such as chamomile and lavender
- Stress ball
- Allergy medicine

— **Discuss with family and co-workers (those whom you feel comfortable with) your emotional challenges.** This doesn't mean saying, "Don't talk to me today! I'm having PMS!" It does mean having a pro-active conversation with those you trust. Let them know ahead of time that there are going to be occasional days when your body isn't functioning at 100%. Tell them you'll let them know when you're feeling less than "excellent" and that you may need to make schedule adjustments. Be very matter-of-fact, not emotional.

— **Acknowledge the fact that home and work may seem more challenging during these difficult days.** On these days you may feel completely overwhelmed by events that would normally be acceptable. Affirm to yourself that the feeling won't last forever.

— **Try to avoid high stress meetings, deadlines, projects, etc. on days that you already know may be difficult.** Remember, lack of concentration and forgetfulness are both in the realm of possible challenges. Plan your days, weeks and months accordingly.

— **Try to avoid "juggling" days during these times.** You know, the days when you plan a morning parent/teacher conference, a lunchtime dental appointment and an afternoon meeting with a very demanding client.

— **Avoid emotionally charged conversations.** This is extremely important. First, if someone says something to upset you, do not respond. Let the person know that you will continue the conversation at a later time. Then take some time to assess the conversation. It is possible that your emotions have distorted your perception of the other person's intent. Second, do not plan conversations that you know may become emotional.

Think of it this way. Most of us wouldn't even consider planning challenging tasks in the middle of the night. We wouldn't be thinking clearly, we might get confused and we might make a mess of whatever we do. So why would you not take into consideration times during the month when you *know* you are going to feel this way? The managing of emotions is not an exact science, and this is why your plan must be unique to you.

In his book *Emotional Intelligence at Work*, Dr. Hendrie Weisinger says, "If you think of life as a series of situations that require some kind of response, then no situation is inherently a problem. It is the ineffectiveness of your response that makes it so." If you have a need, you must voice it. Recognize how your biology as a woman affects your perception of events. Recognize how your emotions affect your perception of events. And always, always seek solutions. It is this newfound attitude that will change your life.

Chapter Three:

The Challenge of Stress Control

> *"If you want the rainbow, you've got to put up with the rain."*
>
> —Dolly Parton

Gina is frequently "stressed out." In fact, she uses this phrase regularly. When asked what her top five stressors were, she said:

1. *Working with people who don't do their jobs*
2. *Getting the children to day care and then getting to work on time*
3. *Her dirty house*
4. *Her mother*
5. *Traffic*

Then Gina was asked to explain how she feels physically when these events occur. Her response included headaches, red face, faster breathing, pounding heart and knots in her stomach. She is being treated for headaches, high blood pressure and anxiety.

What areas of your life are causing you stress?

Read each of the following questions and circle the appropriate response. When you are finished, add up the total of all of your circled numbers.

1 = almost never   2 = rarely   3 = sometimes   4 = frequently   5 = almost always

1	When my office is a mess and the boss is coming for a meeting, I run around organizing as fast as I can.	1 2 3 4 5
2	When someone makes a mistake I become angry and shout at that person.	1 2 3 4 5
3	I expect my colleagues to pitch in on big projects without being asked/told, and when they don't I get mad and do it myself.	1 2 3 4 5
4	When a car cuts in front of me or tailgates me I feel physically upset.	1 2 3 4 5
5	I have expectations of my friends and family, and when they don't behave as I expect them to I place blame.	1 2 3 4 5
6	When money is tight I blame external circumstances.	1 2 3 4 5
7	When my day doesn't go as planned, I think, *"Why me! Nothing ever goes my way!"*	1 2 3 4 5
8	I am easily irritated by waiting in lines at store check-outs.	1 2 3 4 5
9	I find myself having thoughts like, *"I wish my life was more like my friend Jane's!"*	1 2 3 4 5
10	If I take any time for myself during the day, I feel I must make excuses to others for my behavior.	1 2 3 4 5
11	I have thoughts like, *"I'll be happy when I get another job"* (or insert any other event).	1 2 3 4 5

1 = almost never   2 = rarely   3 = sometimes   4 = frequently   5 = almost always

12	My main goal during a confrontation is to be right, not necessarily to reach a solution.	1 2 3 4 5
13	When others offer me solutions to my problems, my response begins with, *"Oh, that won't work."*	1 2 3 4 5
14	I have difficulty making decisions for fear they will be wrong.	1 2 3 4 5
15	When I feel I have done something wrong I relive the event over and over and/or worry about what will happen the next day.	1 2 3 4 5

Total _____

Analysis—Part I

First, consider your level of stress:

60-65: You appear to have great difficulty managing your stress and are probably not living the life you want to live. Your perceptions of normal, daily life events may be distorted. If you continue on this course you may be at high risk for stress-related illnesses.

45-59: You have some stress management skills, but seem to be having difficulty in many areas. It is important for you to pinpoint the areas causing you stress so that you may learn skills in all areas in your life. Failure to do so may lead you down the path to stress-related illnesses.

30-44: You're on the right track, but still need some help. You may have select areas that are difficult for you to manage. Focus on those areas, and you're on your way to a healthier life!

15-29: You appear to be very effective in managing your stress. You understand the difference between normal life situations and truly stressful events. It is important to recognize your approach to stressful situations so that when times get rough, you will continue to be effective. You are contributing to a healthy life!

Analysis—Part II

Now, consider types of stressors by looking at individual questions. A high score is a 4 or a 5.

Questions 1, 10, 12, 14 and 15: Your stressor might be perfectionism

High scores on these questions indicate a tendency toward perfectionism. You may set unrealistically high expectations for yourself and worry what others will think if you make a mistake. Focus on expecting excellence from yourself, not perfection.

Begin by practicing this phrase: *The desire to be perfect damages my self-esteem.*

Questions 2, 3, 4, 5 and 8: Your stressor might be your expectations of others

High scores on these questions indicate that you may live in a "should" world. You may set unrealistically high expectations of others, and when they don't meet your expectations you are, at the least, annoyed. This is a very destructive thought pattern and causes a great deal of stress. Focus on setting more realistic standards for those around you.

Begin by practicing this question: *What would I like for this person to do, and is my expectation reasonable?*

Questions 6, 7, 9, 11 and 13: Your stressor might be your perception of control

High scores on these questions indicate you may see negative events in your life as being out of your control. Instead of taking steps to improve circumstances in your life you might place blame with other people or circumstances. Focus on finding your own solutions.

Begin by practicing this phrase: *There is always a solution!*

You probably already had some idea of your level of stress. A realization of the areas where you feel stress, however, may be new to you. You will learn techniques to help you manage these areas throughout the rest of the book.

The science of stress

Within the last ten years an entire branch of medicine has emerged called psychoneuroimmunology. Big word. Plain meaning. It is simply the science of the connection between the mind and the body. More specifically, it is the study of the interactions between the nervous system, the immune system, the endocrine system and the mind.

Scientists have known for years that your emotional health impacts your physical health, and vice versa. They have known that when you are under a great deal of stress you are more likely to become ill. They have known that stress accelerates the aging process.

In 2004, researchers at the University of California revealed one astounding piece of information related to stress and the aging of cells. The study involved 58 mothers, ages 20 – 50. Thirty-nine of the women had a chronically ill child. The other nineteen had a healthy child.

The study actually suggests a possible mechanism for the increased aging of stressed cells and they found one bit of information that affects you right here, right now: The women who *perceived* they were under a great deal of stress, regardless of which group they belonged to, had cells that had undergone the most aging! Your *perception* of stress matters.

And this perception *and reaction* to stressful events releases two hormones that can be detrimental to your health and longevity. These two hormones are adrenaline and cortisol.

Adrenaline is responsible for the "fight or flight" reaction you experience when your mind perceives danger. If, for example, you are charged by a pit bull, adrenaline will give you the strength to run—or flight! But if your child is charged by a pit bull, that same adrenaline will give you the strength to fight. It does all this by temporarily altering the balance of your body systems. Your heart rate and blood pressure go up. Your breathing becomes rapid and shallow and your pupils dilate.

Cortisol is responsible for helping you deal with long-term, chronic stress. Serious illness, death of a family member, divorce and lack of food are all issues that cortisol could help you with. It helps to regulate blood sugar, blood pressure and the immune system, and it impacts your frame of mind.

So these hormones are life-saving when they are needed. The problem is, we release them unnecessarily. For example, when was the last time you were in real danger? It has probably been a while. But you probably release adrenaline *daily* when you are angry with a co-worker, your boss, your children or even another driver on the road.

And do you truly have the type of long-term stress that warrants cortisol release? Probably not. But think about what happens when you've had a stressful day.

Many researchers believe that these two hormones, especially cortisol, are responsible for today's epidemic levels of obesity, cardiac disease, hypertension and Type II diabetes. Stress, and our perception of it, is literally killing us!

So what can you do to change your stressors, your perceptions of stress and your direction toward a healthier life? You can create a plan to manage your stress—mind, body and spirit.

My choices to take care of my mind

Self-talk can be either very healing and soothing or very damaging. It's your choice. The feelings associated with stress can be traced to a thought. These stress-producing thoughts typically fall into four categories:

- Martyrdom
- I'll be happy when …
- The grass is greener on the other side
- That won't work

Let's consider each of these.

Martyrdom

Nate and Sam were talking one day at work. They were both under intense pressure. Nate told Sam that once a week he plays golf for a couple of hours to relieve stress. Sam said, "Hey, that's a great idea. Give me a call next time you go. I'd love to go with you!"

Linda and Helen were talking one day at work. They were both under intense pressure. Linda told Helen that once a week she takes a couple of hours to read, take a bath and then nap. How do you think Helen responded? Write your answer here: _____

_____

_____

The typical response many women give? "Must be nice!" Women must take the robe of martyrdom off! It is a weight we do not need to carry. When you use this type of language, it shows that you are not confident and assertive enough to ask for what you need.

Are you a martyr? Complete the following sentences:

1. No one ever helps me _____ at home.

2. No one ever helps me _____ at work.

3. I'm the only one who ever _____.

4. When I need help but am too irritated to ask, I _____

_____.

Try these phrases instead:

1. I really need help with _____.

2. The way I will ask for help is _____.

3. If that doesn't work I will try _____.

4. I am a confident woman deserving of help. I am tired of allowing my emotions to keep me from acting in an assertive manner to get that help.

Feeling like a martyr invites stress. It nurtures stress. It multiplies stress. Take off the robe.

I'll be happy when …

Do you find yourself having thoughts like:

- I can't wait till 5:00 gets here!
- My vacation is in two months. I hope I can make it until then!
- If I can just get through this day, the weekend is almost here!
- Things will be much easier when my kids are a little older.
- I'll be a lot happier when I get a bigger house!

These thoughts all have an implied ending: *Then, I'll be happy!* Make a list of thoughts you have that fall under this implied ending:

I'll be happy when _____.

I'll be happy when _____.

I'll be happy when _____.

I'll be happy when _____.

If you work a 40-hour workweek and don't take a vacation, you spend 2,080 hours per year at work. If you are spending those hours waiting for your happiness to start, you are encouraging a stress-filled life. You spend the other 6,656 hours outside of work. Maybe you are spending those hours waiting for your happiness to start.

It's perfectly normal to look forward to the weekend or vacation or your evenings at home with family and friends. It becomes a problem when you are counting the minutes. Something will always stand in the way of your happiness if you don't walk around it!

- What do I do at work/home that brings me joy?
- Do I have relationships that make me look forward to my day?
- Do I look forward to some social time during lunch?
- Do I enjoy some of my actual job/home duties?
- What behaviors do I engage in that rob me of joy?

Change your thought pattern by doing the following:

- Whenever you find yourself thinking this way, immediately write down what you have to be happy about *now.*
- Keep a current Gratitude List. It should include at least ten things you have to be thankful for:

1.	
2.	
3.	
4.	
5.	
6.	
7.	
8.	
9.	
10.	

Keep this list posted in visible spots at work and at home. Update it on a regular basis, and you'll be amazed at all that you have to be grateful for!

The grass is greener on the other side

The grass might indeed not be greener. In fact, with a negative attitude, the grass will start to die when you get there. Will you bring sunshine, fertilizer and gentle rains to the other side? Or will you bring darkness, disease and drought?

Let's say you work in the mailroom for a large corporation. People are calling you all the time to pick up and deliver. No one ever says hello or goodbye, or please or thank you. No one ever asks you how you are. In fact, most of the time they yell at you! Your "office" is hot and dark. *They* have big desks and windows. You think, *"If only I could have her job! She doesn't know how lucky she has it! I'd never yell at anyone if I had her job—I'd be too happy on the other side!"*

What you aren't able to compare is after-work life. You leave work, go to the grocery store and go home. Then you cook dinner, clean up, bathe the children and put them to bed. Now you're finally ready to settle in, watch a little bit of television and go to bed. Sure, it's late and you're tired. You've been running non-stop all day. It only takes you about thirty minutes of watching your favorite show before you start to fall asleep. It's 11:00 PM.

She leaves work with a briefcase full of papers. She goes to the grocery store and heads home. She cooks dinner, cleans up, bathes the children, and puts them to bed. Now she's finally ready to get back to work. She opens up her briefcase and pulls out the reports she couldn't finish today. She works on them until 1:00 a.m. The next thing she knows, she wakes up with her head on the briefcase on the kitchen table. It's 6:00 the next morning.

Comparing your life to someone else's is a dangerous game. What's important is *you* and *your life*. You cannot determine where the green grass is by watching anyone else. You must know yourself and your values and evaluate choices based on those values.

When you are considering moving to the other side, use the following tool to help you decide:

My top five values are:

1.	
2.	
3.	
4.	
5.	

The reason I don't like my current grass is: _____

_____

_____

The reason the grass on the other side looks greener is: _____

_____

_____

Are there better reasons to move or to stay put?			
Pros of staying put	*Cons of staying put*	*Pros of moving*	*Cons of moving*

Now you can make decisions based on real issues instead of perceived desperation and emotion. No doubt there will be times in your life where a change is a good thing. If so, make it. Just be sure to bring a positive attitude to the other side.

That won't work

Consider the number of times you have spoken to someone about your stress and asked for advice. How often do you respond back, *"Oh, I tried that. It didn't work"*? Or maybe you said, *"Yeah, but ... "*

Ask yourself this very important question: *"Do I want a solution? Or do I just want to complain about it?"*

Hendrie Weisinger presents a very logical way to develop good problem-solving skills in *Emotional Intelligence at Work*. The steps are:

1. Identify and define the problem situation

2. Change your perception of the situation

3. Generate alternative solutions (Brainstorm any solutions that come to mind. Be creative.)

4. Explore different options

5. Define best strategies

6. Evaluate the results

Let's go back to Gina, whom you met at the beginning of the chapter. One of her stressors was traffic. How might Gina solve this problem?

1. The problem is: I-65 is always backed up when she leaves for work at 7:00.

2. Her perception is that people are stupid, construction is stupid and that it always makes her late!

3. Alternatives would be:

   - Leave a little earlier
   - Find a different route
   - Change her work hours
   - Quit
   - Work from home
   - Call the construction company
   - Run into the cars in front of her so they'll at least move
   - Get a motorcycle

4. This is the time to explore the practicality of each solution. Consider the consequences of each action. Of course she cannot run into the cars in front of her. She really doesn't want to quit. She continues looking at each idea.

5. She decides to leave a little earlier each morning. She will try this for one month.

6. At the end of the month, she must evaluate the results. Is she getting to work on time now? Yes. Is that what she wanted? Yes. But. Her attitude is no better because she resents leaving early just to get to work on time.

This is the point where many people give up. The first strategy doesn't always work! You may have to revisit the list and go through the steps again.

Once you have made a choice to stay out of these four traps—Martyrdom, I'll be happy when …, The grass is greener on the other side, and That won't work—you will notice a change in your perception of life events. This change won't take place overnight. It takes time. But once you have mastered it, you will wonder how you ever lived any other way!

My choices to take care of my body

Earlier you learned that each emotion begins with a thought. It is also true that each thought begins with a stimulus. And those stimuli enter your body through your five senses. You may not be aware of the power you have in those five senses. With each one you have the ability to filter out much of what shouldn't go in while at the same time allowing in what is calming and uplifting.

Sight

In a 2006 study of 9/11 and post-traumatic stress disorder, Dr. David Spiegel, professor of psychiatry and behavioral sciences at Stanford University School of Medicine, revealed that "we found that people who had too much media exposure tended to be more distressed afterwards."

What you allow into your brain through your eyes really does matter. Keep a log for one week documenting what you watch and how it makes you feel. Pay attention not only to television, but to nature, other people, traffic or anything else you watch that elicits an emotional response in you. Pay particular attention to what you watch before going to bed. Anything disturbing can prevent you from resting.

After one week you will notice which visual stimuli increase your stress and which decrease it. Now you have a list to post in your home and at work reminding you of ways to use your sense of sight.

Now add these tips to your list.

I should avoid watching:	I should watch as often as possible:

Sound

The effects of music on the anxiety levels of pre-operative patients are well documented. Music is often cited as a nursing intervention for hospitalized patients. It is used in airports and prisons. Teachers use it in classrooms. What you hear has power.

As with sight, keep a log of what you listen to for one week. Write down anything that elicits an emotional response. It could be the loud music you're listening to as you drive in rush hour traffic. It could be the birds in your back yard. Maybe it's the gossip from your co-workers. It could be anything.

Now add these stress reduction tips to your list.

I should avoid hearing:	*I should listen as often as possible to:*

Smell

Smell is a very special sense indeed. Your nose is wired directly to the emotion and memory centers of your brain. This is why smells cause you to actually feel nostalgic, happy, sad, afraid, etc. Because of this, you can use this sense for relaxation. And women have a more powerful sense of smell than men do.

Your assignment is to spend some time finding scents that affect you emotionally. You may use oils, lotions, incense, diffusers, etc. Certain essential oils are particularly known for their emotional effects. Among them are chamomile, sandalwood, lavender, jasmine, rosewood and lemon.

Scents I should avoid:	Scents that relax me:

Touch

As with sound, touch is an often-cited nursing intervention for hospitalized patients. The power of the sense of touch, like smell, is especially powerful for women. You might consider the following as touch therapy: stress balls, sheets on your bed, a warm bath, sitting in the sun, massage, a hug, etc.

Now add these to your list.

I do not like the feel of:	I like the feel of:

Look how your list is growing! And finally …

Taste

The best advice is this: Eat a healthy diet that includes a variety of foods—and drink plenty of water. Remember the old "Food Pyramid"? The USDA has replaced that with something called "MyPyramid." The Web site is *www.mypyramid.gov.* It allows you to plug in your age, gender and activity level, and then it helps you to choose foods that are right for you. So forget the latest fad diet. Talk to your doctor, and just eat right.

Eating right will affect you in more than one way. First, eating healthy will contribute to your physical health. Second, it gives you a feeling of accomplishment that you are doing something to take care of your body.

Remember, as women we have certain health concerns that are unique to us. We have to consider the possibilities of anemia, osteoporosis, breast cancer, PMS, menopause and maybe pregnancy. A good place to start is with the MyPyramid Web site. Here are two other sites directed toward women that might be helpful: *www.womenshealth.gov* and *www.fda.gov.* These both offer concrete suggestions on how to address some of our special needs.

As a general rule, there are certain substances you should avoid. One of these is caffeine, a central nervous system stimulant. The last thing you need when you are under stress is a stimulant. In fact, caffeine abuse can be mistaken for anxiety disorder.

At the very least, take notice of the foods you eat and how they affect you—both physically and emotionally. For example, maybe caffeine makes you feel irritated.

Now add these to your list.

I should avoid these foods:	These foods are good for me:

You now have a personalized "stress-busting" list that you can use each and every day. Post it, use and learn from it!

My choices to take care of my spirit

Spirituality is a very personal matter. In *The Anxiety Book*, Dr. Jonathan Davidson, director of the Anxiety and Traumatic Stress Program at Duke University Medical Center, says, "A hallmark of religious faith is that it enables us to find strength and serenity in the face of fear."

Although definitions of spirituality vary, most include a description of something greater than oneself and having a meaning beyond our immediate existence. It is important to at least recognize your spiritual beliefs and then to act on them.

Ask yourself the following questions:

1. What are my spiritual beliefs? _____

_____

_____

2. How do I practice them? _____

_____

_____

3. Does this practice bring me serenity? _____

_____

_____

4. Do I need to develop my spiritual side more completely? _____

_____

_____

The most important point here is to recognize what impact spirituality has on you and then incorporate that into your personal plan.

Sleep and exercise

Finally, as you become aware of the power of your mind, body and spirit, you will notice some additional benefits—better rest and more energy for exercise. The following are recommendations on sleep and exercise:

- Most experts agree you need at least eight hours of sleep each night. Be aware that caffeine and alcohol can affect your sleep pattern.
- Most experts recommend at least 20 minutes of aerobic activity at least three times a week. Your age, weight, current activity level and interests should all be considered when planning your program. Consult your doctor to get started.

Controlling your stress is a choice, and the choice to do so will tip the balance in your favor. Make these choices each and every day. Your perception of your life and your responsibilities will transform in front of your eyes!

Chapter Four:

The Joy of Relationships

"God gave women intuition and femininity. Used properly, the combination easily jumbles the brain of any man I've ever met."

—Farrah Fawcett

Julie just began working at a local library. The library staff consists of ten people: Six full-time and four part-time. Five are professional librarians and the four part-time are clerks. Then there's Julie. She's the only computer technician. She feels like she doesn't fit in. Most of the time, the staff doesn't talk to her unless they need something. Although she doesn't care to socialize after work, she does feel left out when they all go to lunch and don't ask her.

In her book *When Work Doesn't Work Anymore*, Elizabeth Perle McKenna notes that most of the women in her focus groups want to work in more compassionate environments. They want more time to spend with friends and family. And most want to do more in their communities. These are all relationship issues.

Consider the following findings from the *2006 Workplace Stress & Anxiety Disorders Survey* conducted by the Anxiety Disorders Association of America:

- 51% of respondents say stress and anxiety impact their *relationships* with co-workers
- 43% say it affects their *relationships* with superiors
- 61% of women say workplace stress affects their personal *relationships*, particularly with their spouses
- 53% said that interpersonal *relationships* are a major cause of stress
- 44% of women say they cope by talking to family and friends; only 21% of men reported this as a coping strategy

We want relationships. We value relationships. In fact, we *need* relationships. But how do we balance our time? Three ways:

1. First, you must prioritize and assess your current relationships

2. Next, evaluate the time you are spending on those relationships

3. Finally, you have to take action

Step I: Prioritize and assess

The first step is to prioritize your current relationships. On the following list, place the number 1 by the relationship you consider your top priority, number 2 by the second, etc. The most common are listed, with several blank lines for you to add others if you need to.

Prioritize relationships:

_____ Co-workers

_____ Spouse

_____ Parent(s)

_____ Sibling(s)

_____ Friends

_____ Children

_____ Other family

_____ _____

_____ _____

_____ _____

Now consider your attitude about each of these relationships. Which relationships do you value? Be honest with yourself. For the following six statements, place a check mark by all that apply. Don't check that you enjoy a particular relationship if you truly do not.

✓	Co-workers	Spouse	Parent(s)	Sibling(s)	Friends	Children	Other family	Other
I enjoy this relationship.								
I spend the right amount of time on this relationship.								
I should spend more time on this relationship.								
I would like to spend more time on this relationship.								
I wish I didn't have to spend time on this relationship.								
This relationship is draining to me.								

One word I would use to describe this relationship:

Co-workers _____   Spouse _____

Parent(s) _____   Sibling(s) _____

Friends _____   Children _____

Other family _____   Other _____

Step II: Evaluate your current relationships

Now it's time to see if your current actions match up with your priorities. Track the minutes you spend each day with each of the above groups. Make sure the minutes you count are quality minutes. For example, doing the dishes with your spouse doesn't count unless you are relating on a personal level at the same time. And, yes, arguing (although not recommended) does count! Do this evaluation for at least one week.

	Mon.	Tues.	Wed.	Thurs.	Fri.	Sat.	Sun.	Total minutes
Co-workers								
Spouse								
Parent(s)								
Sibling(s)								
Friends								
Children								
Other family								

- With which group did you spend the most time? _____
- The least time? _____
- Is this typically how your week goes? _____
- Does this line up with your priorities? _____
- Does this line up with where you want your relationship minutes allotted? _____

Guilt can come from a discrepancy between what you say you value and the way you are living. We don't, however, always know what we value. Sometimes we think we *should* value a relationship when we really don't. How do you resolve what you value and how you're living?

Step III: Take action

The biggest problem we often face is simply overcoming the idea that there are no choices. That we *must* spend time with this person or we *should* commit more energy to that person.

Of course, sometimes we must or we should. But these terms are usually self-imposed forms of perfectionism. In reality, if we are parents, we must devote a substantial amount of time to our children. If we are spouses, we should make time to be together.

Here are five key categories of relationships and recommendations for each:

Remember that your regular 40-hour workweek commits nearly one-fourth of your total annual hours to work and, of course, to time spent with your co-workers.

Consider Julie's relationship issues from earlier in the chapter:

- Have you ever experienced this type of scenario? _____

- Which side of this scenario might you fall on: Julie's or her co-workers'? Explain. _____

  _____

- Considering that we are social beings, do you regularly isolate yourself or feel isolated during lunch times? What do you do during this time? _____

  _____

- If so, does this help or hinder your attitude at work? Explain. _____

  _____

When you feel a sense of camaraderie at work it affects your attitude about being there. It becomes more a part of who you are and less a burden you have to carry.

Spouse

Be careful not to base your relationship completely on *He does … She does*. Relationships are about more than equality of housework (although this certainly does have an impact!). This can be a vicious cycle: The more household burden you feel, the less time you want to spend with your spouse. The less time you spend with your spouse, the more the communication about the household breaks down.

- Acknowledge that the two of you may never see housework in the same light. Men are not wired the same way we are. They truly can walk through a room and not notice that they have to step over ten piles of laundry.

- *Plan a date night and stick to it!* Comments like "We haven't gone out in years! Who has time?" tend to fall in the martyr category. Women especially "suffer for the cause." We will selflessly sacrifice our relationships with our spouses because that's what we think society expects us to do. This is not expected, it is not healthy and it will only lead to more unhappiness.

- Make this date night about everyone. Plan something special for your children to do at the same time. When you all come back together at the end of the evening you can spend time talking about the fun night.

- You, your spouse, your children and your job will all benefit from this night. You and your spouse will strengthen your relationship. Your children will learn the value of nurturing a marriage. You will feel better the next day at work.

Children

Of all our relationships, this is the one you *must* commit to. Because of this, the relationship can be viewed as a burden. How can you work on this challenging relationship?

- Correct any thought distortions. Children *do* require attention and time. They *do* need you. They *do* learn from you. They *will* try your patience—*each and every day!* The relationships with your children will be the first to throw you into the guilt trap. But they don't have to!

- Schedule time each and every day to do something personal with your children— even if it's just 15 minutes. Make sure it is something you both enjoy. For example, if you hate video games, don't schedule that on a regular basis. You will dread it, resent it and forget about it! Don't berate yourself if occasionally it doesn't happen. What matters is the long term.

- Expect the unexpected. If you have children, you *will* hear, "Oh, I have a project due tomorrow." Then you ask, "How long have you known about it?" only to hear "A month." If this happens on a regular basis, you might want to consider consequences. But the reality is, it will happen from time to time. What do you do? Be prepared. Create an "Emergency Project" box. Have items like paper, markers, glue, craft supplies, binders, etc. (alter the box as your children get older). Look at this "late night" together as quality time. And have a list of "surprise treats" you can do for yourself during this time. Listen to your favorite CD while you're doing it. Make your favorite tea. Sure, you'll both be tired in the morning, but this is not a forever.

- Or, you can "teach them a lesson" by not helping. They will have to suffer the consequences of their procrastination. The point is, there are choices. Make one and move on.

- Change how you look at your week. As you look at your planner (I'm assuming you have one; if you don't, get one), notice what thoughts are going through your head. Are you thinking, "Oh my gosh, it's going to be a stressful week. Cindy has a soccer game, Bobby has a dentist appointment and Lindsey has a project due! My life is crazy!" Change that thought pattern. After all, there are 168 hours in a week. Chances are, these three events will take maybe five of them.

- At the beginning of each week ask yourself, "What are my parental responsibilities this week? This will be great time to spend with my children." Children are not your burdens, they are your blessings and your responsibilities. As long as it's reasonable, the schedule of events is just part of life.

Other family members

Because of our ability to nurture, many women feel the need to care for everyone. You probably don't want to let anyone down. You may feel responsible for everyone in your life. Remember that as a grown woman, you are now responsible for yourself and, if you have one, for your own family. That doesn't mean you abandon your extended family, just that you schedule time for them.

Friends

Much of what we said for family goes for friends as well, so it doesn't need to be repeated. There is, however, one major difference: You can choose your friends! And you *should* choose.

- Friendships are important to women. You can talk to your friends about your spouse, your family, your children and your co-workers. Study after study shows the link between quality friendships and health. So how do you manage the time?

- As before, schedule the time. Of the 168 hours per week, surely you can schedule one for a friend. Talk to your family about the positive impact it will have on you, and then let them see it! Choose times that are convenient for you. What about meeting for an early coffee? It's a choice!

- Instead of avoiding phone calls because you are too busy, consider saying this: "I'm so glad you called! I have five minutes before we sit down to dinner. What's going on?" Better yet, make a pact with your friend about how you will manage phone calls. It's a choice!

- What about those "needy" friends? Are you letting them negatively impact your life and the lives of those around you? If you're not quite ready to "cut the cord," consider calling them once a week and saying, "I have five minutes before I have to leave and just wanted to call and say hi." It's a choice!

How can you create relationships that work for you? Try these five simple ideas:

1. Understand that you will not like everyone you work with.

2. Understand that not everyone will like you. Not as easy!

3. Plan some social functions during office hours—like a covered dish luncheon (if this fits your work environment).

4. Make it a goal each day to have a short conversation with someone. If you work for a large business, maybe you could meet someone new once a week.

5. Initiate some type of personality testing. Knowing this information will help employees to communicate with and understand each other better.

Relationships are really a large part of what we are referring to when we speak of balance. In her book *Reinventing Ourselves After Motherhood*, Susan Lewis reinforces this idea by finding that "When a woman leaves or scales back her career to be at home, one of the most difficult adjustments can be with respect to friendships." Cultivating these relationships gives us a reason to go to work and a reason to come home. Remember this as you seek balance.

Chapter Five:

The Gift of Communication

> *"A woman is the full circle. Within her is the power to create, nurture and transform."*
>
> —Diane Mariechild

Allison is a recently divorced mother of two children, ages one and seven. She has been teaching at a local middle school for six years and is having a difficult time juggling her duties at work and at home. Her principal views her new single status as a time for her to pick up some extra commitments at school. After all, now that she's "alone" she probably needs to keep busy. The problem is that Allison has enough to keep her busy and is feeling overwhelmed. She doesn't want to say no to her new assignments for fear it will make her look less than dedicated. She stays after school every day to fulfill her commitments. Her lesson plans are suffering. Her day care costs are rising. Her house is in disarray. She feels trapped, stressed and frustrated. And her children, family and friends miss her.

By nature, women are communicators. On average, research suggests that we talk almost three times more than men, with women speaking 21,000 words per day and men only 7,000. Some researchers believe this is due to the effects of testosterone on the brain of the male fetus, while others believe it is due to gender socialization.

Dr. Luan Brizendine suggests in *The Female Mind* that women devote more brainpower to talking and speak more quickly than men and that we release "feel good" chemicals when we talk.

But *how* are we communicating? *What* are we communicating about? Four areas of communication can impact your sense of balance. They are:

1. Being positive when you speak

2. Being able to ask for what you need

3. Being able to say no

4. Being assertive in your approach

Being positive when you speak

Research suggests that up to 80% of our thoughts are negative. This certainly translates into negative speech. It is a vicious cycle with broad consequences:

- Diminished sense of balance
- Release of harmful stress hormones
- Negative influence on those around you
- Damaged relationships

We don't say to ourselves, "Today I'll be as negative as I possibly can be. This will be an effective way to deal with my problems." But if you're not careful, you can easily fall into the negativity trap. How can you avoid the fall? By examining your style and making adjustments as necessary.

Do a self-evaluation: Are you a positive or a negative person?

Examine the following words:

Insulted	Controlled	Lonely	Stressful	Guilty
Embarrassed	Confused	Afraid	Awful	Impossible
Offended	Discouraged	Intimidated	Angry	Failure
Trapped	Ignored	Terrified	Frustrated	Miserable

- Write down each time you use these words or other negative words
- Write down the event associated with the use of the word
- Write the entire sentence you spoke
- Write down a new sentence that is more positive

For example:

Word(s): Awful and miserable

Event: This week I have to work with a woman who is very difficult to get along with.

Sentence: *This week is going to be awful! That woman will make my life miserable!*

New: *This week will be challenging! I will grow and develop new skills as a result of this week. I know I can handle this because I am a smart, confident woman!*

You don't always have control over the events that come your way. Life events are what they are—sometimes positive, sometimes negative. But you always have choices when you respond.

Let someone else evaluate you

Get a communication pal. This is slightly more challenging than self-evaluation because you have to be prepared for feedback from another person. But it is *very* effective. This pal can be a friend, spouse or co-worker—anyone you trust and spend considerable time with.

Make it simple—no complicated feedback forms! Simply say, "I'm trying to take control of my life and make some changes. One of these changes is to be a more positive person, and I could really use your help with that! Would you let me know when I'm being negative? I promise I won't be offended." Come up with a signal. Perhaps your pal could tug an ear when you're being negative. You might be very surprised at the number of tugs you see in a day!

Putting it all together

One week should be sufficient to get an idea of your level of negativity. At the end of this time, ask yourself the following questions:

- Do I see myself as a negative person?
- Do others see me as a negative person?
- Are there particular words and/or phrases I commonly use?
- How do I feel when I say them?
- Was I able to replace these words and/or phrases with more positive responses?
- How did I feel when I responded in a more positive manner?
- Could positive communication be part of the puzzle of a more balanced life?

At first, it's sufficient to simply notice when you are being negative. Trying to eliminate it altogether might be overwhelming and cause you to give up. You might also find your friends and family making less than favorable comments about your sudden change. Remember, misery loves company. Once you find yourself noticing on the spot, it's time to implement changes. Small steps toward a new life.

What about Allison? Can she change the fact that she has children? No. Can she change the fact that she just went through a divorce? No. Can she change the fact that she is now financially responsible for her family? No. Can she take steps to improve her circumstances? Absolutely! And can she change the way she speaks about it? Definitely!

Now, continue working on that positive speech! You'll be amazed at the impact it will have on you *and* those around you.

Being able to ask for what you need

There was a TV commercial from the 1980s for Enjoli perfume. It went like this: "I can put the wash on the line. Feed the kids. Get dressed. Pass out the kisses and get to work by 5 of 9. Cause I'm a woman—Enjoli! I can bring home the bacon. Fry it up in a pan. And never, never, never let you forget you're a man! 'Cause I'm a woman—Enjoli!"

We all laugh now. But is the Superwoman mentality still popular? If you buy into it, then yes, it is.

This mentality feeds into the common fear of asking for what you need. Consider the following advice for women's issues:

- *Ask* for help with household chores and nighttime feedings. *Ask* your husband or partner to bring the baby to you so you can breast-feed. (On postpartum depression)
- *Ask* for help—let others know how they can help you (On single and married working moms)
- We need to learn how to *ask* for help (On middle-aged women caring for children or aging parents or both)

You need to ask. Not asking often puts women into the martyr category. And, again, this never works. How many times have you heard, thought or even said, "Well, if I have to *ask,* then it's not worth it!" Go back to the section on the differences between men and women (especially if the asking involves a man). Just remember, they're wired differently and may not pick up on your need. *You* have *not because you* ask *not!* But, *how?* How do you ask for what you need? Take these steps:

- Decide *what* you want
- Look at the possible consequences of your request
- Analyze why you won't ask
- Script and carry out the request

What do you want?

Amidst the daily struggles that come along with work and home, you may forget to put thought into what you really want. To really begin seeking a solution. What would make your situation better? Who can help you? Often the answer is hidden in sarcasm or "wishful thinking."

For example, Allison would often say to her close friends, "I just *love* sitting at my desk grading papers during my planning time! It gives me plenty of time to worry about everything *else* I have to do!" *Translation:* Allison would like to use that time for other responsibilities. When she took time to evaluate what she wanted, she realized she wanted to leave during some of her planning time and then grade papers at home after her children went to bed.

Think of how some of these statements translate well into a need or want:

Gee, thanks for all your help with the time sheets!
Translation: I need help with the time sheets.

I wish I could have two weeks off at Christmas. You're so lucky!
Translation: I'd like more time off around the holidays.

This pile of dirty dishes is certainly a beautiful addition to our décor!
Translation: I would like for someone to do the dishes.

It must be nice to stay home all day and volunteer for every committee your school has.
Translation: I would like to do more at my child's school.

After identifying what you need or want, begin to analyze why you won't ask for it. This is crucial before moving on.

Why won't you ask?

Answering this question often reveals a great deal about the way you view your life. You might find out if you're incorporating your values into your life by asking yourself the following questions:

- Did I think of this option before?
- Am I afraid?
- If so, what am I afraid of?
- Does being overwhelmed make me feel important? If so, does the feeling of importance outweigh the feeling of stress?
- Do I think I might appear weak?
- Does asking go against my desire to be perfect?
- Do I feel like I should be able to do it all?
- Do I enjoy staying angry with those whom I believe are not helping me?

Allison's reason is fear. She believes it might jeopardize her job if she asks to have a flexible schedule. "After all," she thinks, "no one else asks for special privileges." What Allison doesn't think about is the fact that companies across the country offer flex-time benefits. Maybe by asking, she can open up new opportunities for other teachers.

Identifying your reason for not asking allows you to then evaluate whether the reason is valid or not.

Possible consequences of your request

The best way to evaluate your concerns is to make a pro/con list. This allows you to then make a decision as to how you will proceed. If the cons truly outweigh the pros, you might decide that pursuing your need or want is not realistic—at least at this time. The key is this: If you do decide not to make a request, you must accept it and move on—no resentment. If you decide to make a request, you must confidently move forward.

Use the following examples to help guide you when making your list:

Allison would like to leave during her planning time two days per week. She will finish grading papers and planning lessons at home.

Pros	Cons
I will be able to take care of appointments during the day	I will have to work at night at home
I will be able to do some volunteer work at my children's school	I will miss out on some of the group planning sessions at work
My stress level will go down	My principal and other teachers might think I can't handle my job responsibilities

Karen needs someone to do the dinner dishes on a regular basis.

Pros	Cons
I will not be angry anymore	I might have to remind them
Other family members will learn to be responsible	My children might not get their homework done

Based on the pros and cons, decide if your request is worth pursuing. If so, you are now ready to script your request.

Script your request

This is where you get rid of emotional phrases and replace them with assertive phrases. Here are seven important points to remember:

1. Be positive.

2. Use "I" statements to explain your feelings.

3. Be specific and ask for what you want—no beating around the bush or hinting.

4. Avoid use of the word "but." (This is a great job, but there's something I'm unhappy about.)

5. Explain how this issue affects you now as well the benefits of the change.

6. Confirm understanding.

7. Follow up and evaluate.

Examples:

Allison could say: "Mrs. Jones, I love teaching here, *and* I love being a mom. As you know, I have some new responsibilities in my life now. It's been challenging to do everything, so I've come up with a solution. I'd like to suggest a flex-time schedule as a trial for the next three months. During this time I will leave during my planning time two days a week. On those days I'll complete my work responsibilities at night so I won't get behind. Will this work for you?"

Karen could say (after a family evening together): "Isn't it great when we have time to relax together as a family? It's hard sometimes because there's so much to do around here. And sometimes I feel like it all falls on my shoulders, and then I get frustrated and yell. So I have a solution. I made a "Kitchen Duty" calendar for the next month. Each person is assigned a week, and it will be that person's job to make sure the dishwasher is unloaded and loaded and the garbage is taken out. This will also make everyone more aware of cleaning up after themselves in the kitchen and we'll all be able to spend more time together. Does everyone understand?"

Will this always work? No. Will people have to be reminded? Yes. The important point is that you said what you wanted, and now you have to keep a positive attitude and continue to remember that you always have choices.

For example, what if Allison's boss says no? Should she run home, fall into bed and feel that she's tried and there's nothing more she can do? No, of course not. She still has choices. She can accept it. She can try again—maybe with some more details and facts. She can think of a different arrangement. And, ultimately, she can look for another job and quit.

What if Karen's family agrees enthusiastically and then constantly forgets it's their week? Should she say, "Forget it! I'm the only one who ever does anything around here!" No, of course not. She also has choices. She can accept it and do kitchen duty herself. She can continue to remind. She can try another method. She can implement punishments. There are always choices.

Try this one:

Linda would like for her best friend to stop calling her after 9:00 at night. In fact, she'd prefer to talk before her family is all home at 6:00. She's already tried being the one to make the phone call so that she's sure it will happen early. But that didn't work. Her friend still calls her late. Linda is frustrated.

_____

_____

_____

_____

Now that you've learned how to script a request, it's time to learn to say no to others' requests!

Being able to say no

The following titles are from books about saying no:

- *How to Say No Without Feeling Guilty: And Say Yes to More Time, and What Matters Most to You*
- *When I Say No, I Feel Guilty*
- *Don't Say Yes When You Want to Say No: Making Life Right When It Feels All Wrong*

Interesting. Do you really need an entire book to be able to say no? Maybe. Maybe not. Begin by asking yourself these questions:

- How often do I say yes when I really want to say no?
- How do I feel when I do this?
- Why do I say yes?
  - I'll feel guilty
  - I'm afraid
  - They won't like me
  - They need me
  - What will I miss out on if I say no?
  - Will I still be important?

Once you've decided you'd like to be able to say "no" more, there are two steps to take:

1. Deciding when to say no

2. Actually saying no

Deciding when to say no

Each time you are faced with the choice of saying yes or no, use the following phrase:

"I am saying yes to _____ *because it's more important*
than _____ *."*

For example, Candace is asked to work late for the third time this week. This is happening more and more frequently, but she never says no. Never. Her boss never asks her on Mondays and Thursdays because he knows she takes classes on those nights. Tonight she is feeling exhausted and is beginning to feel resentment about this new schedule. This could be her statement if she says yes:

"I am saying yes to working overtime because it is more important than my rest and happiness."

Remember to check the values that you identified earlier. And the same rules apply as when you were deciding whether or not to make a request. If you decide to say yes, then you must do it without resentment. If you decide to say no, then you should prepare for the consequences.

Actually saying no

Believe it or not, the best way to say no is to not really say no at all. In Meryl Runion's book *PowerPhrases*, she teaches a technique called ACT. It stands for:

- *Acknowledge* the request
- Explain your *circumstances*
- *Transform* your no into a positive statement

So what could Candace say? She could say, "Mr. Smith, I understand it's important to you that the X project is completed on time. Because I worked late Tuesday and Wednesday, this is my only night to work on my home and school responsibilities. I'd be glad to stay late one night next week. Which night would you like for me to work?" (The positive doesn't always mean you have to do something. It could be as simple as saying, "I hope next time I can help you out.")

Again, this will not *always* work. And when it doesn't, it's important to remember that you always have choices. Try this one:

Trish loves being a grandmother! But she also still has a very demanding job as an account manager. She is very involved in her church and also volunteers at the local animal shelter. Lately she is growing weary of babysitting any time her son and his wife want to go out. Often they call at the last minute when Trish is very tired. She hasn't said no because she feels like they might think she doesn't love the grandchildren.

A_____

C_____

T_____

So far you've learned to be positive when you speak, ask for what you want and say no. The final piece to the communication puzzle is being assertive.

Being assertive

Actually, everything you've practiced and learned so far is part of assertive communication. Now you simply need to be ready to implement what you've learned. This involves examining and modifying your nonverbal mannerisms and practicing.

You may already know the three basic communication styles: Passive, aggressive and assertive. As these styles apply to issues relating to balance, here's what they look like:

In order to get what I need at work and at home, I ...		
Passive	**Assertive** *(where you want to be)*	**Aggressive**
Don't do anything	Focus on the issue	Scream
Overreact	Evaluate what I need	Demand
Suffer in silence	Evaluate what others need	Become sarcastic
Hint	Focus on solutions	Intimidate
Hope	Script out a request	Nag
Get defensive	Use a confident voice	Huff and sigh

How do you get to the center column? How can you come across as an assertive communicator? You've already learned the verbal message. Now work on the nonverbal one.

Most experts agree that 93% of the message you are sending during communication is nonverbal. This includes your tone of voice (including pitch, volume and pace) as well as your body language (including posture, facial expressions, gestures and eye contact). Recall Karen's request for help with kitchen duties. Read the request out loud:

> *Isn't it great when we have time to relax together as a family? It's hard sometimes because there's so much to do around here. And sometimes I feel like it all falls on my shoulders, and then I get frustrated and yell. So I have a solution. I made a "Kitchen Duty" calendar for the next month. Each person is assigned a week, and it will be that person's job to make sure the dishwasher is unloaded and loaded and the garbage is taken out. This will also make everyone more aware of cleaning up after themselves in the kitchen and we'll all be able to spend more time together. Does everyone understand?*

Now practice in the mirror with the following modifications:

- Use a higher-pitched, louder voice, emphasizing the words "I" and "my"
- Use a sarcastic tone and wave your arms broadly as you talk
- Speak very softly and slowly while looking down, as if you are not making eye contact
- Say it with a smile
- Say it while slouched over with a frown

Now practice using the tone, pitch, volume, pace, expression, posture, etc. that you believe relays your message in a confident, assertive manner.

Continue to practice, first in the mirror and then with someone you trust. If you are not used to using your confident mannerisms in front of another person, you might be surprised how your words come out for the first time. Make sure that first time is with someone safe—someone who will give you great feedback and help you prepare for your new life of balance!

Chapter Six:

The Curse of Perfectionism

> *"My theory on housework is, if the item doesn't multiply, smell, catch fire, or block the refrigerator door, let it be. No one else cares. Why should you?"*
>
> —Erma Bombeck

Erma Bombeck (1927-1996) was best known for her humorous look at the role of the housewife. During her years as a writer, she wrote 14 books including the best-sellers *The Grass is Always Greener Over the Septic Tank* and *I Lost Everything in the Post-Natal Depression.* She also wrote for magazines and newspapers and traveled the speaker's circuit for many years. She was talented.

Erma began her writing career in junior high school for her school newspaper, *The Owl.* It was obvious she had talent. In high school she wrote a regular column for her school newspaper. Praise abounded. She even interviewed Shirley Temple for the city newspaper, *The Daytona Herald.* College was a different story for Erma. She barely passed first semester freshman composition, and the newspaper articles she submitted were repeatedly rejected. She was not perfect.

When Erma and her husband adopted their first child, she was filled with excitement! But she was immediately overwhelmed by the amount of work that was required. She was tired, lonely and confused. She thought she was doing a terrible job and that something was wrong with her. She wondered why she wasn't perfect.

As she continued to write, she became more popular and more in demand. Her trips took her away from home more often and for longer periods of time. She was losing her balance. She examined her life and her career and made changes where she could. She made choices.

Perfectionism

Even if you don't consider yourself to be a perfectionist, you probably have tendencies to be. Think about it. If you didn't, you would probably "let more things go" and feel less pressure. And, you probably wouldn't be reading this book!

It is not okay to giggle and smile as you say, "Well, yes, I *am* a perfectionist! That's just the way I am." It's not okay to say that with the belief that it means you have high standards. That it makes people look up to you. It's time to stop believing that giving up perfectionism means giving up your credibility.

You do not have time to be perfect. Period. You are a member of a generation of women trying to do it all. It's challenging enough to just get it done, much less to do it perfectly. This chapter gives you permission to be less than perfect. It gives you permission to be excellent at some things, good at others, rotten at a few and even give up many.

So what's the big deal? So what if you want to do a great job? So what if you have high standards? Consider these statistics:

- According to a study published in *American Journal of Psychiatry*, approximately two-thirds of the adult women subjects with anorexia and one-third of the patients with bulimia reported perfectionism in childhood
- According to a study at University of Southampton in the UK, perfectionists are more likely to develop irritable bowel syndrome (IBS) after an intestinal infection

Dr. Randy Frost of Smith University in Massachusetts has come up with six categories of perfectionist behavior, along with descriptions and possible consequences. People may have traits in some or all of these categories:

1. Concern over mistakes

This type of perfectionism relates to a fear of what people might think. These people become so fearful when they make a mistake that they are unlikely to come forward, and may actually cover it up. Imagine the possible consequences of this type of perfectionism in fields such as medicine. If a nurse tried to cover up an error, the result could be fatal.

2. Personal standards

These perfectionists set unrealistic expectations for themselves. Believe it or not, this can actually sabotage the very goals they set. They may procrastinate a task if they feel they will not meet their own expectations.

3. Parent expectations

Many perfectionists are actually striving to meet standards set by their parents. These people spend very little time pursuing their own goals and are often left unsatisfied with their careers.

4. Parental criticism

Like people who live by their parents' expectations, these perfectionists live to avoid criticism. They may also live a life filled with unmet personal needs.

5. Doubting of actions

The problem these people experience typically comes at the end of a project. They cannot "give it up" and move on. They feel sure something was left undone. So procrastination isn't really the problem here; instead, it's meeting final deadlines. Indecision is also very common with these perfectionists.

6. Organization

Often when we hear the word "perfectionist," we think of someone with a neurotically neat office and home. But this is just one dimension of perfectionism and probably stems from one or more of the other categories. These people are meticulous and picky about everything they do and they make sure everything is in its place.

So perfectionism is multi-faceted. It may be a result of the way you grew up and your self-esteem, and it is often driven by fear of failure. In fact, a major difference between perfectionists and high-achievers is the driving force behind behaviors. Perfectionists are motivated by fear of failure, while high-achievers are driven by a desire for success.

What are some other consequences of perfectionism at work? It can:

- Keep you from leaving work at work
- Keep you from forming relationships that increase your satisfaction at work
- Damage current relationships
- Keep you from feeling pride in your work
- Keep you from making changes (asking for a promotion, leaving a position)

What are some consequences of perfectionism in other areas of your life? It can:

- Keep you from enjoying time at home
- Keep you from looking forward to home time
- Keep you from participating in activities you enjoy (like hobbies)
- Damage friendships
- Keep you from cultivating new friendships

The following phrases tend to precede perfectionist thoughts:

- Why can't I … ?
- I can't believe I …!
- What if I … ?
- I should have …
- How could I have … ?

When you find yourself having one of these thoughts, write down the following information:

1. This event is causing me distress: _____

   _____

2. This is what I'm afraid might happen—is it likely to happen? _____

   _____

3. This is the worst-case scenario—is it likely to happen? _____

   _____

4. If this worst-case scenario happens, what will I do?_____

   _____

5. Is there any background evidence to support this happening?_____

   _____

6. What is the best-case scenario? _____

   _____

7. What positive thoughts can I use to replace my concern?_____

   _____

Example:

Connie conducts financial planning seminars for a variety of companies as an independent contractor. Her biggest client, Company X, sends her availability calendars six months in advance. It is her responsibility to send in the calendar with her available dates and to then keep the company up to date on any changes. In the year that she has done work for them, this has worked well. This month, however, she discovered she had made an error. She forgot to inform them of a change in her calendar, and now she's double-booked.

Here's how Connie might analyze her thoughts:

1. The event that is causing me distress is having made an error in my scheduling. How could I have forgotten to inform Company X that I had a change in my calendar and was no longer available for those three days in June?

2. I'm afraid Company X will no longer trust me because of this mistake. I've always been very organized so far, so this is not likely to happen. I'm also afraid the scheduling assistant will "scold" me when I tell her. This may happen. After all, what do I expect? Do I think she should say, "Oh, great! That's wonderful! Thank you so much!" No, she'll probably be annoyed because it makes her job more difficult.

3. The worst-case scenario is that they will no longer contract with me. This is the first mistake I've made in a year. The participants are very pleased with the seminars. This is very unlikely to happen.

4. If this were to happen, I could accept more dates from other clients. I'd also understand that it would be for the best. After all, do I really want to work with a client who dismisses me for one error in a year?

5. There is no evidence to support this happening. They are reasonable, professional people.

6. The best-case scenario is that they will be forgiving of my first error without scolding or consequences.

7. I could think, "I am human and I will make mistakes. I will accept whatever consequences come my way and learn from this."

It is admirable to achieve excellence in your endeavors. It is not, however, admirable to strive for perfection. It is not attainable. It damages your self-esteem. It damages your productivity at work and at home. And it damages your relationships. Practice this thought, and you will be on the road to excellence: *I want my life to be fulfilling and productive. My desire for perfection is actually preventing me from living this life. I will therefore strive for excellence in all that I do. When I fall short, I will learn. Each of these learning experiences will eventually mold me into a wise person.*

Guilt

The Merriam-Webster dictionary defines guilt as "the fact of having committed a breach of conduct especially violating law and involving a penalty." Make a list of circumstances in your life that cause or have caused you guilt. List as many as you need to, and write your list in complete sentences:

1. _____

_____

2. _____

_____

3. _____

_____

4. _____

_____

5. _____

_____

Now notice how you phrased your sentences. You may have written something like, "I feel guilty when … " It is very interesting that most of us include the phrase "feel guilty." Read and compare the following stories:

Melanie works as an administrative assistant for a large chemical company. After completing a chemical analysis report for a well-known client, she realized she made an error in one of the tables. She typed in the wrong numbers in one of the "percent pure" columns. Melanie was embarrassed by her error and said nothing. When the client found the mistake, the laboratory was blamed and the lab technician was written up. Melanie still said nothing, but she felt guilty about it.

Lauren is a training manager for a health care company. She designed a new program that significantly improved the way training is delivered to the company's six offices across the country. Her program was approved, the budget was in place and Lauren hired six new trainers. All was well. Six months later she learned that the CFO severely mismanaged funds, and her program was cut. Lauren had to lay off the six new trainers. She felt guilty and dreaded having to talk to each of the trainers.

They both felt guilty. But only one of them was. Which one? Melanie. Her error was not the issue. She was guilty because she tried to cover it up, and in doing so, allowed another person to take the blame. Lauren, on the other hand, had done nothing wrong. Through no fault of her own her program was terminated, along with six employees. She was not guilty.

Feeling guilty doesn't really make a lot of sense. By definition, you either *are* guilty or you *aren't*. But is it really that simple? The cases of Melanie and Lauren are pretty clear-cut. But what about your guilt over not calling your mother as often as you think you should? Are you guilty? Well, that depends. Remember your values assessment. Sometimes you may feel guilty due to a discrepancy between what you say you value and how you're actually living. Guilt in this case can be a signal that you need to make some changes in your life.

You are not alone. What are some common reasons women feel guilty?

- In November 2006, *Babytalk Magazine* and the March of Dimes released a study on the emotional effects of premature birth on mothers. According to the study, 64% of moms felt guilty for the early delivery, even though they realized it wasn't their fault.
- An October 2006 survey conducted by the BBC found 41% of women feel guilty about putting their pre-school children in day care.
- *Perspectives on Labour and Income* (a publication of Canada's National Statistical Agency) released a study about the effects of caring for an elderly relative or friend. They studied working women who also provide at least one daily hour of elder care. The study found that over 40% of these women feel guilty.

The usual suspects: Motherhood, daughterhood, sisterhood, wifehood, friendhood, employeehood—and the list goes on and on. Women tend to take on the problems of all the people they have relationships with. And then we feel miserable. It seems like a dichotomy, but it really isn't.

Women are wired to be nurturers. To have relationships. To nurture those relationships. To help. We tend to feel good when we are in positive relationships. But this doesn't mean we are responsible for everything. And when we allow ourselves to feel guilty about issues that aren't our responsibility, what we're really doing is allowing our real responsibilities to go unmet.

Consider this scenario:

> *Nancy is married, works full-time, has three children ages 3, 7, and 10 and is very active in her church. Nancy's sister Donna has made some bad choices in her life. She dropped out of high school after a battle with drugs. She married a man who won't work. She has two children, and she works part-time. Donna calls Nancy constantly to either complain about her life or to ask for help. Nancy and Donna actually have a close relationship, but there are problems. When Donna calls, the conversations can last an hour or more. Nancy's husband urges her to end the call, but she feels guilty because Donna needs her. Sometimes Donna calls to ask for money. She makes comments about how "lucky" Nancy and her husband are because they have a nice house and other things. Nancy doesn't tell her husband, but she sometimes gives Donna money because she feels guilty for having so much while her sister has so little.*

In her mind, Nancy is doing the right thing by listening to and helping her sister. After all, they are sisters. But Nancy's true responsibilities lie with her husband, her children, her job and her church. She is not responsible for the choices her sister has made, as sad as they are. The long phone calls take time from Nancy's family. Her money would be better spent on her own family.

Every person you meet in life has some kind of responsibility, whether to a husband, wife, children, parents, job, church, etc. We all have them. We are not responsible for other people's responsibilities. They are.

This doesn't, however, excuse us from helping family and friends (and sometimes even strangers) at all. Sometimes we *are* guilty if we don't help. Use the following tool each time you are questioning your responsibility to someone outside of your immediate family. It is filled out with Nancy's issue as an example.

Am I responsible to help?

I feel guilty when: My sister calls to talk about her finances, and I don't feel like I can tell her I have to go.

What life value can I relate this issue to? Responsibility.

Is the issue part of everyday life that everyone has to deal with? Yes. We all have to take care of ourselves and our families and pay our bills.

Is the issue out of the ordinary? Something the other person can't or shouldn't have to bear alone? No. She has had money problems for as long as I remember. This is not new.

Am I responsible? No.

What are my *choices* in dealing with this issue? I can continue to let her take control of my life. I can never speak to her again. I can talk to her about the impact her situation is having on my life. I can take small steps to limit the amount of time I give her.

Which *choice* will I make? _____

_____

_____

Once you open yourself up to the possibility of choices you will be better equipped to deal with the issue. You are never *made* to feel guilty. You have the choice. If you feel guilty, it's because you *choose* to feel that way. Make your decision, and let go of the guilt. If you decide you are responsible, then help—and still let go of the guilt. Your decision has been made.

What if the issue is not outside your world of responsibility? What about the guilt over placing your child in day care? Not spending enough time with your husband? Obviously you can't say, "Well, I'll just let that one go." It is still about choices, and you can still use a similar tool:

I feel guilty when: I have to drop my son off at day care when I go to work.

What life value can I relate this issue to? Responsibility.

Is the issue part of everyday life that everyone has to deal with? Yes. We all have to take care of ourselves and our families and pay our bills.

Is the issue out of the ordinary, or something I can't or shouldn't have to bear alone? Somewhat. My husband should also help in this area.

Am I responsible? Yes.

What are my choices in dealing with this issue? I can accept that I have to/want to work and focus on the positive things that come from my work. I can quit my job. I can consider work options that will allow me to be more flexible and spend more time with my son. I can consider options that include my husband and/or other family members.

Which *choice* will I make? _____

_____

_____

The bottom line is this: We always have choices. There are always solutions. Finally, as you try to resolve your feelings of guilt in your life, ask yourself these harsh but life-changing questions:

1. Am I the type of person who would rather complain than seek a solution?

2. Does guilt make me feel important?

3. Do I enjoy the attention I get when others know how guilty I feel?

Be honest, and then be ready for a new life with less guilt.

Chapter Seven:

The Realities of Getting It All Done!

*"Now I sit me down to plan. I have a pencil in my hand.
If it should break before I'm done, I pray I find another one!"*

—Tami West

You may feel you have so much to do that your pencil cannot take that much writing! The most important point to remember as you work on managing your time is to have the right attitude. Each time you prepare to manage your time, say one or more of the following phrases. Modify them so that they fit your particular situation:

- I am a strong woman
- I am not afraid of hard work
- As a human being, I am designed to work hard
- Every person on this planet has a load to carry
- I also have a load to carry
- My load includes (insert your responsibilities here)
- I will carry my load joyfully
- I will carry my load with dignity
- I will be proud of how I manage my load
- I am a smart woman
- I will now prepare for my day
- It is not realistic to believe that everything will fall into place
- I must plan to make that happen

How are you managing your load?

Read each of the following statements and circle the appropriate answer:

1 = rarely   2 = sometimes   3 = often   4 = almost always

I am late to meetings, appointments, family events, etc.	1 2 3 4
I have trouble finding my keys when I get to my car	1 2 3 4
People make comments like, "I don't know how you find anything on that desk!"	1 2 3 4
I overbook myself and schedule too many appointments in the same day.	1 2 3 4
I work late at night trying to finish household chores.	1 2 3 4
I find myself looking up the same phone numbers, addresses, e-mail addresses, etc. over and over.	1 2 3 4
I find myself starting a new task before finishing what I am currently working on.	1 2 3 4
I have more than one "to do today" pile on my desk.	1 2 3 4
The items on my "to do" list don't get done.	1 2 3 4
I pick up the same piece of paper multiple times without making any progress.	1 2 3 4

Answers with scores of 1 and 2 are probably not your problem areas. None of us is perfect. Focus on those areas with scores of 3 and 4. Equally important is to understand what the questions mean:

- Questions 1, 4, 5, 7 and 9 involve time management skills
- Questions 2, 3, 6, 8 and 10 involve organizational skills

Of course the two are related, but you may be able to see trends. Let's focus first on time management.

Managing your time

This section really involves using the skills you've already learned in prior chapters. For example:

- You will manage your time well if you are guided by your values
- You will manage your time well if you are able to say no
- You will manage your time well if you recognize the importance of relationships
- You will manage your time well if you expect excellence, not perfection
- You will manage your time well if you are able to manage your emotions
- You will manage your time well if you are able to ask for help
- You will manage your time well if you see the end result as less stress

But how do you fit it all in? By investing time up front. Commit a week of your life to self-analysis and planning. Your work for one week of your life will pay off for the rest of your life. Here are the four steps to successfully managing your time:

- First, analyze how you are spending your time
- Second, determine what stays and what goes
- Third, determine what can be delegated and delegate properly
- Finally, determine what must be done by you and plan each day

Step I: Time analysis

Make copies of the "My Time Quadrant" form on the next page. Keep several at work and several at home. A clipboard is a great way to use this tool. Any time you work on a task, no matter how small, write it on the grid. Do this for one week. An example is included. Consider some of the tasks listed below:

Work	Home
Making copies	Cooking
Faxing	Washing dishes
Returning e-mails	Cleaning kitchen
Returning phone messages	Cleaning bathrooms
Filing	Vacuuming
Sorting mail	Dusting
Scheduling meetings	Laundry
Attending meetings	Shopping
Speaking with customers/clients	Making/driving to appointments
Phone conferences	Sports games/practices
Budget reports	Yard work
Time sheets	Caring for animals
Daily planning	Paying bills

My Time Quadrant

Tasks that are important to me:

Task	Payoff
1.	
2.	
3.	
4.	
5.	

Tasks that are important to others:

Task	Payoff
1.	
2.	
3.	
4.	
5.	

Tasks that are important to me and others:

Task	Payoff
1. Fax contract to client.	We both understand agreement
2.	
3.	
4.	
5.	

Tasks that appear to be important to no one:

Task	Payoff
Stacking mail on table for children even when I know it's junk	None

Now answer the following questions:

1. Does your grid look balanced?

2. If not, which quadrant or quadrants are tipping the scale?

3. Is this fine with you, or do you see the need to make a change?

4. Do you have many tasks for which there are no payoffs (consider that the payoff may be in the future)?

5. Why are you still doing these tasks?

6. Do you have many tasks in the quadrant labeled "Appear to be important to no one"?

7. If you do, why are you doing these tasks? Is there a hidden importance?

Step II: Spring cleaning

You may have heard the story about the homemaker who always cut the end of the ham off before placing it in the baking pan. When asked by her daughter why she did this, she replied, "I don't know except for the fact that my mother always did it that way." Later, while talking to her mother, the woman asked, "Mom, why did you always cut the end of the ham off before placing it in the baking pan?" Her mother replied, "Well, that's the way your grandmother always did it." So the woman went to see her grandmother and asked, "Grandma, why did you always cut the end of the ham off before baking it?" She replied, "Because that's the way my mother did it." The woman really wanted to know, so she went to ask her great-grandmother. "Great-grandma, why did you always cut the end of the ham off before placing it in the baking pan?" Finally, there was an answer. "Oh that's simple, dear, the hams were always too big for my small pan. I cut the end off so it would fit."

It's time to get rid of or modify those tasks we do again and again for no reason. The easiest and best way to do this is to write them down along with a plan to get rid of them.

Copy the following page so that you will have one for work and for home. An example is included.

The task to be eliminated	Plan to eliminate it	Plan to modify it
1. Stacking junk mail for children	Place ALL mail for children in one basket. Tell children it is their responsibility to check it daily. I will throw away all contents of basket each Friday.	

The task to be eliminated	Plan to eliminate it	Plan to modify it
1.		

Step III: Delegation

You've gotten rid of unimportant tasks. Now it's time to decide what to do with the rest. Each item left in your grid needs to be evaluated, and this can be done very quickly by asking yourself these four questions.

1. Is there someone else who would enjoy this task more than I do?

2. Is there someone else who would be better at this task than I am?

3. Is there someone else who should be doing this job instead of me?

4. Is there something I could do for someone else in exchange for their doing this task?

Now make your plan. As before, copy the page so that you'll have one for work and one for home.

Example:

Dorothy is annoyed when it's her morning to pick up the newspapers from the front desk and distribute them to individual offices. Each person in the department has his or her assigned morning for this task. Dorothy always forgets. It's important for the departmental supervisors to have these papers each day.

The task to be delegated	Possible people to ask	The plan
Picking up the morning newspapers	Linda Ellen Joann	Ask Linda first. She comes in early every morning anyway and says she doesn't mind when it's her day. I can separate the mail for her when it's her day to do it. I don't mind, and she hates it.

The task to be delegated	Possible people to ask	The plan

Remember when you delegate a task to give the person the proper tools to carry it out. Do this no matter who you are delegating to—children, assistants, co-workers, spouses, friends, etc. A common pitfall in delegation is to let the task go, only to find out the person hasn't followed through or isn't doing it properly. Then you may be inclined to think: *I knew it wouldn't work! I'll just do it myself!*

Delegating properly will help to ensure success. Include the following information any time you let go of a task:

1. Give clear, concise directions.

2. Provide the proper tools necessary for success. This includes budget if necessary.

3. Schedule time for feedback and evaluation.

Delegation is a crucial part of being a successful manager of your time. There are, however, many tasks that you will have to do yourself. These are part of your load.

Step IV: Managing your load

What's now left in your grid is yours. Begin your plan by analyzing the tasks you do frequently—maybe daily or even weekly. Consider the examples provided.

Task	How I handle it now	Is this effective? If no, why?	More efficient way
Checking e-mails	Every time I hear the ding	No—I get distracted from work every five minutes	Close e-mail or turn sound off. Check mid-morning and mid-afternoon.
Doing laundry	On Saturday	Yes, this works	
Grocery shopping	Practically every day to get what I need for that day's dinner	No! I spend too much time there	Plan meals each week, make a list and go to the store once—on a weeknight when it's not crowded

Here's a blank one for you to use:

Task	How I handle it now	Is this effective? If no, why?	More efficient way

Now you're ready to plan! If you don't already have a planner (paper or electronic), you should certainly get one. Find one that works for you. Consider a planner with the following features:

- Small enough to fit in purse or briefcase
- A "month-at-a-glance" page with a tab for each month
- Behind each month, a page (or at least a section) for each day of the month

When using a planner, try these tips:

- Always write phone numbers down with appointments on your month view
- Using a highlighter, color code appointments by category; for example, children's sports in pink
- Keep phone numbers, e-mail addresses and addresses in the sections provided
- Using self-adhesive labels or tape, affix frequently used shipping addresses, phone numbers, etc. to the inside cover of the planner
- Keep your to-do list on the individual day pages provided

Following these steps will keep a record of information you might need six months down the road.

But how do you make that to-do list? Begin by creating an all-inclusive list of everything you think you will, should or want to do. One at work might look something like this:

All-inclusive list

- Make reservations for sales trip
- Archive old files
- Reschedule strategic planning meeting
- Confirm vacation plans
- Update performance reviews
- Recruit new regional assistant
- Read mail backlog
- Approve vendor invoices
- Feed office plants
- Enroll in dental insurance
- Birthday card for boss
- Sign up for HR training
- Write monthly reports

Put this list in a protective plastic sleeve and post it in a convenient location—wherever you sit to plan your day. Use this each time you make a to-do list.

In his book *Productivity Power*, Jim Temme provides a wonderful formula for prioritizing your day and actually using your list— I x U = S. Using the familiar concepts of Important and Urgent, it involves ranking your tasks by importance as well as by urgency. Important tasks are those that relate to the vision you realized in chapter one. Urgent tasks are those that must be done soon, regardless of their relation to the mission of your life. Using numbers, you assign a rank to each task.

So, how is it done? Using some of the tasks listed above, it might look like this:

1. In the "Today's Activities" section, list all of the tasks that need to be done.

2. Rank the importance of each task in the "Rank/Value" column; 1 is the most important.

3. Rank the urgency of each task in the "Time Value" column: 1—must be done today; 2—can be done soon; 3—can be done anytime.

4. Multiply the "Rank/Value" column number by the "Time Value" column number and record this in the "Raw Score" column.

5. Finally, give each task a Priority Rank with the lowest scores identifying the tasks to be done first. When you have a tie, simply choose, based on the lower Importance score, which should be done first.

Today's activities	Rank/value importance (1= most important)	Time value 1 = urgent, today 2 = timely, soon 3 = flexible, anytime ok	Raw score	Priority rank
Make reservation for sales trip	1	2	2	1
Birthday card for boss	2	1	2	2
Sign up for HR training	1	3	3	3
Approve vendor invoices	2	2	4	4
Read mail backlog	2	3	6	5
Feed office plants	3	2	6	6
Archive old files	3	3	9	7

Other tips for an effective to-do list:

- Try to choose at least one task from your all-inclusive list that isn't a priority that day. This will help you to accomplish the "shoulds" and the "wants."
- Do not cheat when assigning values.
- Spend no more than 10 minutes planning your day.
- Make your work list before you leave work each day. This will help your brain to be at ease at home instead of worrying about what you have to do the next day.

Finally, remember this: You are managing YOUR time. The choices you make are yours. No guilt. No anger. No worries. No stress. This is your load. You are an intelligent, capable woman. You are ready!

Organizing your space

Consider the following statistics:

- According to the National Demographic Society, Americans waste over 9 million hours each day looking for things
- According to *Office World News*, the average executive wastes 150 hours per year looking for documents
- Getting rid of clutter in the home could eliminate up to 40% of housework
- A Harris Interactive poll found that 23% of adults pay bills late because they lose them

And not only that, clutter and disorganization make you feel bad. Think of the last time you organized a desk or cleaned out a closet. How did you feel when it was finished? How can you keep it that way? By using the same approach in organizing your space as you did in organizing your time. It requires the same mental commitment and offers the same payoff.

There are four steps to successfully arranging your space:

1. First, assess what type of stuff you have.

2. Second, decide what stays and what goes.

3. Third, decide what stuff other people can manage.

4. Fourth, decide what to do with the stuff you keep.

Step I: My stuff

A "Clutter Quadrant" is an excellent way to assess your "stuff." The key to successful use of this tool is planning. First choose a manageable area to arrange and have this tool ready. An area can be as large as you feel you can handle at one sitting. It can be as small as arranging your purse! The following example involves arranging a desk.

My Clutter Quadrant:

Things I need	Things others need
Computer	
Lamp	
Standing files	

Things we all need	Things no one needs
Stapler	Basket with old potpourri
Hole punch	Wooden ruler
Phone book	

Now ask yourself these questions:

1. Were your quadrants balanced?

2. If not, which quadrants tipped the scale?

3. Is this fine with you? If no, do you want to make a change?

4. How many items did you have in the "Things no one needs" column?

5. Why do you still have these items?

Step II: More spring cleaning

First, deal with the "Things no one needs" column. Before getting rid of these items, ask yourself these questions:

1. Why are you holding on to this item?

2. Is it fear that you might need it later?

   • How likely is this?

   • How long has it been since you've used the item?

   • Would it be costly to replace should you need it later?

3. Consider any other reasons you might be holding on to these items.

Now what? It's time to part ways with items that really need to go. Donations are usually appreciated. Consider schools, nursing homes, animal shelters, neighborhood centers and the many charitable organizations out there. Just remember, some stuff is truly junk and should be thrown out!

Step III

Now that you've gotten rid of items that no one in your family or at work needs, what do you do with the rest? Just like tasks, decide which items you will take responsibility for and which can go to others. Work with two columns: "Things others need" and "Things we all need." Use the tool below.

Item name	Why it is in current location?	Is this the best place for this item?	If no, where would be a better home for it?
Stapler	My desk because I use it the most	Yes	
Hole punch	My desk because that's where it landed when we bought it	No	On my son's desk. He uses it more than I do.

This is the part where you get to give away "gifts" to your own family or to the people you work with. Just like you don't have to do every task yourself, you don't have to take care of every item yourself.

Step IV

Now you're down to stuff that is truly yours. It's your responsibility. What are you going to do with it? For each item you've decided to keep, collect the following information. Now you have an Item Locator that you can update as needed. Example provided is for a desk.

Item	How often do I use it?	Do I need it close at hand or stored in a drawer, closet, box, etc.?	Where is it and should I move it?	If I should move it, to where?
Stapler	Daily	Close	Desk—No	Desk
Mailing envelopes	Maybe once every two weeks	Stored	Desk—No	Under desk in box
Invoice file	Weekly	Close	Desk—Yes	On my desk in stand-up file
Calculator	Daily	Close	Desk—No	Desk
Reference notebooks	Twice a year	Stored	Under desk— Yes	Storage box in closet

The act of writing down placement of your items forces you to evaluate what you use, how you use it and how to store it most efficiently. It also provides a locator for those items you decide to store. No more trying to remember *Now where did I put that?*

Finally, here are 25 tips for organizing your space and time and getting some balance to your life:

1. Trade your "in" box for a tickler file. Depending on your needs, you can get one with one pocket for each day of the month or each day of the year. As soon as you touch a piece of paper that needs attention at a later time, place it in the appropriate slot. Check the file daily.

2. Keep keys, cell phone, pens, lipstick, etc. in the same place in your purse or briefcase. Even if it takes a few extra seconds to return it, it will save you time the next time you need it.

3. Keep frequently used files in a stand-up file on your desk.

4. Arrange your desk so that items you use regularly are within reach.

5. Have a designated area on your desk completely clean for use as a work area.

6. Purchase a "full-spectrum" light bulb for your desk lamp. The wavelength most closely mimics natural sunlight.

7. Personalize your work area enough to feel comfortable.

8. Notice your multi-tasking habits. Ineffective habits involve doing more than one activity that requires brain-power. An example would be listening to a co-worker at your desk while you continue to compose an e-mail. Effective multi-tasking involves doing one brain activity at a time. For example, you could have a book to read while you wait in line at the store.

9. Schedule time for relaxation on your to-do list.

10. Keep a voice recorder in the car to dictate ideas immediately.

11. Take a speed-reading course.

12. If you return phone calls in the car, use a hands-free system.

13. Keep a voice recorder handy. That way if someone gives you something like a phone number you can dictate it instead of writing. Be safe!

14. Notice your "peak" productivity time. If you're a morning person, schedule your high-energy tasks for then.

15. If you don't keep your to-do list in your planner, keep it in a notebook so that you can refer back to details when you need to.

16. Make folders in your e-mail program to file messages. Twice a year delete what you don't need, and store the rest on a CD.

17. If you have multiple people in your family (especially children), assign each person a separate colored towel. Store or get rid of the rest. Your laundry loads will decrease dramatically.

18. Let each person be a "chef" for one night each week or month. Forget perfectionism. Even young children can assemble ham sandwiches and veggies for everyone! This takes work from you and gets the family involved.

19. Consider using a meal-planning service.

20. Purchase laundry hampers with a "darks" side and a "whites" side. Now your laundry is already sorted.

21. Decline the bags at stores for single or large items. Now you don't have to worry about storing or throwing away the bag.

22. Keep extra bags under the current bag in the trash can. Now when you empty one you have another ready to use.

23. Combine housework with exercise. The benefits? You won't feel as burdened, you'll get into shape and your house will look great!

24. Make shopping time a night out. Go out to dinner with a spouse or friend and then swing by the grocery store with a list. By this time the stores will be empty, and you will look forward to it. If you have children, plan something special for them that night too.

25. Finally, remember the tremendous brain power of other women. Draw ideas from co-workers and friends. And do this on a regular basis. Great ideas are generated every second, so make yourself open to them. And make sure to share yours with others.

Chapter Eight:

Looking Ahead

> *"On vacations: We hit the sunny beaches where we occupy ourselves keeping the sun off our skin, the saltwater off our bodies and the sand out of our belongings."*
>
> —Erma Bombeck

Sun, saltwater and sand are inherent to the beach. Challenges are inherent to the life of a working woman. No more avoiding them. It's time to meet them head on! This chapter is filled with the final reminders and tools for achieving a sense of balance in your life.

Here's what research has projected about the future lives of women:

- A 2006 study conducted by the U.S. Department of Labor, Women's Bureau, found that women comprised 46% of the total U.S. labor force and are projected to account for 47% of the labor force in 2014

- The study also found that women are projected to account for 51% of the increase in total labor force growth between 2004 and 2014

- An AARP study found that 44% of women 45-55 years old had at least one elderly parent and one child less than 21 years of age living at home. The term given to this arrangement is the "Sandwich Generation."

- According to the U.S. Census Bureau, the fastest growing segment of the population is those 65 and over. They are projected to comprise approximately 17% of the population by 2050 compared with 7% in 2002. Consider the impact this will have on women as caregivers.

Recall two books discussed in Chapter One: Betty Friedan's *The Feminine Mystique* and Elizabeth Perle McKenna's *When Work Doesn't Work Anymore*. Women will continue to grow in the workforce. Women will continue to grow in their responsibilities at home. McKenna stated perfectly that, "it is up to us to create change." That's why you are working through this book.

You have examined your nature as a woman, your relationships, your emotions, your methods of communication, your tendencies toward perfectionism and stress control and your methods of time management and organization. What do you do now? What if you need to make significant changes in your life? As you finish evaluating the balance in your life, it's time to set some larger goals.

Looking toward my future

Recall your personal and work visions from Chapter One. What will you be doing six months from now? One year? Five years? Use the following tool to restate your vision and plan your goals. Remember these six important tips when you are setting your goals:

1. Always write down your goals. This act is a powerful step toward success!

2. Set goals in five areas of your life:

   - Family
   - Professional and Financial
   - Physical and Health
   - Spiritual and Intellectual
   - Community and Friends

3. Make the goal positive.

4. Break the goal down into specific steps.

5. Set a time.

6. Evaluate at the time you have set and make revisions if necessary. Be sure to evaluate any revisions.

My plan for success

My personal/professional vision: _____

_____

_____

My goal is: _____

_____

_____

The steps I will take to accomplish this goal are: _____

_____

_____

I will meet this goal (time): _____

_____

_____

Evaluation of my goal: _____

_____

_____

Example:

My goal is: To work part-time in my current position with my current employer

The steps I will take to accomplish this goal are:

- Discuss my desire with my husband and my supervisor
- Look at other employees who work part-time in a position similar to mine and collect information from them about their successes and challenges
- Plan a budget that will include my new reduced income
- Pay off two credit card bills
- Gradually work fewer hours to ease into the new schedule

I will meet this goal: Within six months

Evaluation of my goal: At the six month mark, I have discussed with husband and supervisor, spoken with other part-time employees and implemented a new budget. I still need one more month to pay off the credit card bills, so my new deadline is one month from today.

Evaluation of revision: I am now working part-time. The budget is working. My supervisor is pleased. My husband is happy that our home is being managed. My stress level has decreased. I am pleased.

Sometimes our goals will take us right where we thought they would. Great! But not always. And when they don't, we try again. The key is to try. You've heard it before: Change will happen.

"Certainty? In this world nothing is certain but death and taxes."

—Benjamin Franklin

What keeps us from making changes?

One word—fear. In his 1943 paper *A Theory of Human Motivation*, Abraham Maslow proposed his now famous Hierarchy of Needs. He proposed that as human beings we all have the same basic needs.

Our fears, then, will fall into one of these categories:

1. Fear of anything that threatens our basic survival needs

2. Fear of losing our financial security

3. Fear of losing friendships, friends or family

4. Fear of losing respect or losing our position in society

5. Fear of not growing intellectually, emotionally or spiritually in life

How do you overcome these fears? By converting them from fears into situations that need resolutions.

Situation	Fear and basic need it entails	Situation	Possible solution
I would like to work flex-time	I will have no money to retire on—this is a fear of losing my financial security	If I work flex-time, I will not have the same retirement benefits	Make an appointment with the benefits coordinator to discuss my options

When you do this, your decisions are not longer based on fear, but rather on knowledge.

You are not alone

As you journey through your life as a woman, remember that you are not alone. Women all over the globe are seeking the same thing you are—peace of mind! You have support. You just have to seek it with your entire being.

Companies are beginning to recognize the value in providing work/life benefits to all employees, including women. In its November 2006 issue, *Working Mother Magazine* highlighted its "Hall of Fame" companies when it comes to these benefits. Here's what some of America's top corporations had to say:

> *Citigroup launched a global flexible work initiative in the fall of 2005, and since then more than four thousand employees in thirty-five countries have already submitted flexible work plans. Through strategies like this, we hope to foster a work environment that helps employees meet their professional and personal goals.*
>
> —Charles Prince, CEO and Chairman, Citigroup, Inc.

> *Flexibility in when and where work gets done will become a necessary staple—not an accommodation. In this global economy of 24/7 work, employees will need more autonomy and tools to assist them in managing workloads. Employees' needs change in the different cycles of their work and lives. As the saying goes, "It's not your father's company anymore." Well, it's also not your father's workday and work style anymore.*
>
> —Mark Loughridge, SVP and CFO, IBM Corporation

> *To retain the best and brightest talent, we must foster a work environment that supports greater quality of life. At Marriott International, a variety of programs is available, including flexible schedules, child care and a twenty-four-hour toll-free number that provides referral services, confidential advice and counseling for work and personal life concerns.*
>
> —J.W. Marriott, Jr., Chairman and CEO, Marriott International, Inc.

It's out there if you want it.

Final thoughts …

Remember, laughter and hope are healing, so when you feel you can't go on, come back to this page of all the quotes from previous chapters—plus some! Now, take a deep breath, and keep moving! Happy travels!

"Once you get a spice in your home, you have it forever. Women never throw out spices. The Egyptians were buried with their spices. I know which one I'm taking with me when I go."

—Erma Bombeck

"I'd much rather be a woman than a man. Women can cry, they can wear cute clothes, and they are the first to be rescued off of sinking ships."

—Gilda Radner

"A woman is the full circle. Within her is the power to create, nurture and transform."

—Diane Mariechild

"If you want the rainbow, you've got to put up with the rain."

—Dolly Parton

"God gave women intuition and femininity. Used properly, the combination easily jumbles the brain of any man I've ever met."

—Farrah Fawcett

"Women who seek to be equal with men lack ambition."

—Timothy Leary

"When I stand before God at the end of my life, I would hope that I would not have a single bit of talent left, and could say, 'I used everything you gave me.'"

—Erma Bombeck